Read Write In

Literacy and Language
Anthology

5

Janey Pursglove and **Charlotte Raby**

Series developed by **Ruth Miskin**

OXFORD
UNIVERSITY PRESS

OXFORD
UNIVERSITY PRESS

Great Clarendon Street, Oxford, OX2 6DP,
United Kingdom

Oxford University Press is a department of the
University of Oxford. It furthers the University's
objective of excellence in research, scholarship,
and education by publishing worldwide.
Oxford is a registered trade mark of Oxford University
Press in the UK and in certain other countries

© Oxford University Press 2013

The moral rights of the authors have been asserted

First Edition published in 2013

British Library Cataloguing in Publication Data
Data available

ISBN: 978-0-19-849376-1

10 9 8 7 6 5

Paper used in the production of this book is a natural,
recyclable product made from wood grown in sustainable
forests. The manufacturing process conforms to the
environmental regulations of the country of origin.

Printed in China by Imago

Acknowledgements

Cover illustration by Alexandra Huard

Illustrations by: Maria Christina Pritelli; Andrew Painter;
Andres Martinez Ricci; Paul McCaffrey; Mike Phillips; Martin
Sanders; David Semple; Victor Tavares

The publishers would like to thank the following for the
permission to reproduce photographs: **p14r**: OUP/Ingram;
p15tr: ekler/Shutterstock; **p15br**: OUP/Photodisc; **p14 & p15**:
Photography by Hardwick Studios/www.hardwickstudios.
com; **p26 & p27**: MEN syndication; **p28**: James Carmichael JR/
NHPA; **p29**: Ingret/Shutterstock; **p30tl & tr**: Peter Macdiarmid/
Getty Images; **p30bl**: Leon Neal/AFP/Getty Images; **p30br**:
Matt Cardy/Getty Images; **p34**: Hemis/Alamy; **p35** from left:
Ann & Steve Toon/NHPA; Piotr Skubisz/Shutterstock; Vladimir
Chernyanskiy/Shutterstock; **p37t**: Felipe Rodriguez/Alamy;
p37m: Can Balcioglu/Shutterstock; **p37b**: Blend Images/
Alamy; **p50 & p51**: Charles Shearn/Penguin Group; **p52t**:
Jeremy Strong 1996/Nick Sharratt 1996/Penguin Group; **p52b**:
Jeremy Strong 2005/Seb Burnett 2005/Penguin Group; **p53t**:
Jeremy Strong 2007/Penguin Group: **p53b**: Jeremy Strong
1997/Nick Sharratt 1997/Penguin Group; **p54 & p55t**; With
kind permission from Anthony Horowitz; **p55b**: Cover from
THE FRENCH CONFECTION written by Anthony Horowitz,
Cover illustration © 2007 Martin Chatterton, Reproduced by
permission from Walker Books LTD, London SE11 5HJ, Cover
from STORMBREAKER, SKELETON KEY, ARK ANGEL written by
Anthony Horowitz, Cover designs © 2005 Walker Books LTD,
Boy with torch logo ™ & © 2005 Stormbreaker Productions Ltd,
Reproduced by permission from Walker Books LTD, London
SE11 5HJ; **p64**: North Wind Picture Archives/Alamy; **p66t**:
WaterFrame/Alamy; **p66b**: Mark Mitchell/Rex Features

Background Images by: Perov Stanislav/Shutterstock; Kirill R/
Shutterstock; Shcherbakov Ilya/Shutterstock; Darryl Sleath/
Shutterstock; Phant/Shutterstock; Dgrilla/Shutterstock; OUP/
Brand X Pictures; OUP/Pixtal; OUP/Imagebroker; OUP/Ingram;
OUP/Corel; Apollofoto/Shutterstock; Nosha/Shutterstock;
Albo003/Shutterstock; Gala/Shutterstock; Angela Jones/
Shutterstock; Restyler/Shutterstock

The authors and publisher are grateful to the following for
permission to reproduce copyright material:

Pie Corbett p31 'Goodnight Stroud' from *The Apple Raid:
Poems for Year 6* chosen by Pie Corbett illustrated by Lydia Monk
(Macmillan Children's Books, 2001), reprinted by permission
of the author. **The Irish Post p26** 'Bravery Award for Fire
Hero Boy', The Irish Post, March 2009 at: www.irishpost.co.uk,
reprinted by permission of The Irish Post. **Andrew Fusek
Peters p32** 'Last Night, I Saw the City Breathing' from *The
Moon is a Microphone: The wild and wacky poems of Andrew Fusek
Peters* (Sherbourne, 1997), reprinted by permission of the
author. **Jeremy Strong p38** 'this is NOT a fairy tale', copyright
© Jeremy Strong 2003, first published in *Kids' Night In* (Collins,
2003), reprinted by permission of David Higham Associates.

We have made every effort to trace and contact all copyright
holders before publication. If notified, the publisher will rectify
any errors or omissions at the earliest opportunity.

The authors of the Fiction texts in this Anthology (excepting
those listed above) are as follows: **Janey Pursglove p4**
Prometheus and Pandora, text copyright © Oxford University
Press 2013; **Jon Blake p16** *Bling!* text copyright © Oxford
University Press 2013; **Gill Howell p56** *Dragon Slayer*, text
copyright © Oxford University Press 2013; **Lou Kuenzler p70**
Father's Day copyright © Lou Kuenzler 2013; Lou Kuenzler has
asserted her right under the Copyright, Designs and Patents
Act 1988 to be identified as author of this material.

The authors of the Non-fiction texts (excepting those listed
above) in this Anthology are as follows: **Adrian Bradbury
p12** 'How to Write Instructions'; **p13** 'How to Write a Greek
Myth'; **p14** 'Have a go at…Chocolate Chip Ice Cream'; **p28**
'Newshound'; **p34** 'Meet the Monster!'; **p36** 'Meet the Future!';
p50 'Jeremy Strong Biography'; **p54** 'Anthony Horowitz
Biography'; texts copyright © Oxford University Press 2013;
Charlotte Raby p30 'Beach Bonanza!'; **p64** 'The Kraken'; **p67**
'A Dragon Spotter's Guide to the Chinese Lung Dragon', texts
copyright © Oxford University Press 2013; **Janey Pursglove
p79** 'The Big Debate', text copyright © Oxford University Press
2013

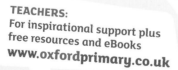

Contents

Prometheus and Pandora

Janey Pursglove

① *The gods of Ancient Greece had amazing powers. They could conjure thunder storms, change their shape and bring the dead back to life. They could create and then crush whole kingdoms, all in an instant. You might think that with all those powers you would never be bored or jealous or, well, silly. Unfortunately, the gods were often all of these things. Of course they were also immortal, so perhaps they had too much time on their high and mighty hands as well...*

*Zeus was king of the gods. He had the whole sky and the heavens as his kingdom. He filled it with his colossal body and his mighty voice, firing off thunderbolts from the ends of his fingers and setting fire to whole cities if he felt like it. Zeus never got a bit bored, quite annoyed or a little jealous. Everything about Zeus was big – massive – **gargantuan**!*

Mount Olympus was home to all the gods. Many stories tell us about the lives they led there. They can also tell us about ourselves...

② Earth was once a cold, dark, miserable place. It was empty of all human or animal life; silent as a tomb except for the whispering winds that blew across its dusty plains. The sun was hidden behind dark clouds so it was always night. It had air and water but no fire to create warmth and light.

While this pitiful planet spun on its axis, Prometheus, cousin of Zeus, was filling one of his endless days by making a little figure out of clay. He made it look like a tiny god. He moved its arms and legs and it appeared to dance. He sat it down, stood it up and made it lie down as if it were asleep and somehow he grew to love the little being. Then one day Prometheus blew very gently onto the figure to remove some dust but his godly breath was so **potent**, it woke the clay creature's sleeping soul. Prometheus had breathed life into the first mortal man.

"I have given you the gift of life, so I will give you protection from all harm and evil!" he cried. Prometheus knew that Zeus would never allow a human to live on Mount Olympus. So, he breathed life into more figures, and, with sadness in his heart, he sent them to live on earth – cold, dark and uninviting as it was.

③ Meanwhile, Zeus had been watching Prometheus and was angry with his cousin for giving life to the little creatures without his permission.

'As long as those creatures dwell upon the barren earth and have only the dark of everlasting night and the sound of the wind for comfort, I will not punish Prometheus,' he thought. 'But I fear he has forgotten that his powers are subject to my law!'

Prometheus' affection towards the mortals grew, as did the pity he felt as he watched them struggle to survive on the harsh, bleak earth. Against the wishes of Zeus, who had started to enjoy watching them shrivel and die, Prometheus began to give the mortals gifts to make their lives easier. He had a brother called Epimetheus who always copied whatever Prometheus did. One day Prometheus spied his brother making strange shapes out of clay.

"What are you doing?" he asked. "What are they supposed to be?"

"Each one is called an animal," Epimetheus replied. "Your little men all looked the same. I've made many different creatures."

His fingers pushed, pulled, squeezed and smoothed the mud and once he was happy with the figure, he set it on the ground to dry.

Prometheus picked one up.

"They're all different but they're all called 'animal'?" he scoffed.

Actually, he was jealous. Each one was a completely different shape – they were wonderful. But of course he couldn't say so.

"These are not even finished," said Epimetheus the animal-maker. "I paint them different colours and make patterns on their skin."

He pointed to a pile of finished animals. One had black stripes on a golden background. Another was yellow with brown marks daubed all over it. It had a very long, thin neck, a short body and spindly, knobbly legs. In spite of himself, Prometheus was impressed.

"Do you want me to help you breathe life into these? We could send them as presents for my mortals on earth."

The brothers worked hard to finish the models. They even asked Hephaistos, the god of fire, to speed up the drying and firing process.

As well as the animals, Prometheus had two more special surprises to give to the humans…

Prometheus had stolen a tiny bit of fire from Hephaistos and kept it burning in a reed stalk. He sent this incredible gift to earth. Fire! Now they had warmth and light! The mortals didn't have to shiver in misery anymore.

Man was finally able to see. They could find each other and the animals. They could hunt some of them and cook the meat on blazing fires.

④ Last of all, Prometheus made sure his mere mortals had the gift of language.

"With this gift you can name things in your world," he said. "You can give each animal its own name."

And so they did. Language helped them to describe their world. Animals became tigers, giraffes, deer, antelope. They made up words to talk about what they were feeling and thinking. They sat around the leaping flames of a fire and told each other their adventures and called them stories.

"What a story! I want to remember it forever!" declared a mortal one night. So he made up a system of symbols to represent sounds and words. He carved them onto tablets of stone for all to learn. Every new word was added to the stone store. Every new idea and invention was given a name and its symbols set in stone.

But the all-seeing eyes of Zeus were upon them. Zeus saw the power and knowledge that the mortals were acquiring through the doings of Prometheus and Epimetheus.

'Those pathetic mortals need to be kept in their place,' he thought. 'They have no right to live such comfortable god-like lives! They should go hungry sometimes and show more respect to me, the king of the sky and of thunder.'

He sought out Prometheus. "Prometheus, you have displeased me. You have made men in the image of the gods and given them too much! I demand that from this day, man shall give me the best part of all the animals they hunt for food." Only by this sacrifice would he be **appeased**!

⑤ Scared as he was, Prometheus decided to protect his mortals and show his scorn for such unfair demands.

"It should be the duty of the strong to help the weak. What is power without compassion?" he cried. And he thought, 'Let us see if Zeus' mighty power is stronger than his mighty greed!'

He made two parcels. In one he hid a pile of dry bones beneath thick layers of animal fat. The other, much smaller parcel contained all the delicious, succulent meat off the bones wrapped in the discarded animal skin.

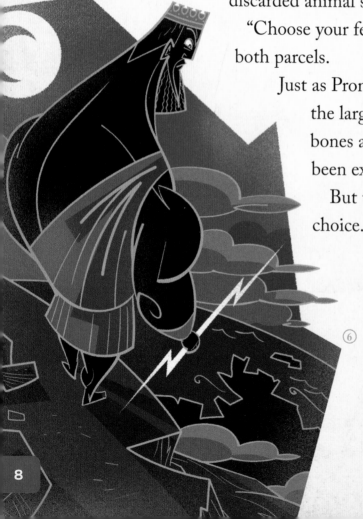

"Choose your feast, Zeus," he said, offering both parcels.

Just as Prometheus had predicted, Zeus chose the larger parcel containing nothing but bones and fat. Prometheus thought he had been extremely clever to trick the great god.

But the true power of Zeus lay in his choice. For he had known exactly what was in each parcel and decided to show everyone how disrespectful Prometheus had been...

⑥ "Fool Prometheus! To think you could outwit me, the king of all gods! Now all of Olympus can see what a treacherous little wretch you really are! See what delight I shall have in taking my revenge."

In that instant, Olympus became bathed in a dazzling light. And at the very same moment, earth was plunged into darkness. Words froze on the lips of all men on earth as they were sucked back into the cold darkness of ignorance and silence.

⑦ "Prometheus, your punishment will match my fury!" Zeus roared. "You are like a fly to me, I could pull off your wings for my pleasure and crush you with one finger. Your endless suffering will be my eternal pleasure!"

Prometheus was seized and chained to a rock. At sunrise an eagle flew towards the captive. Zeus commanded the eagle to gnaw at Prometheus and eat his liver.

Zeus then told poor Prometheus, "Each night, your liver will regrow and so your punishment will be repeated for all **eternity**!"

But Zeus was determined to punish Epimetheus too, and with him *all* mankind. Next he asked Hephaistos to take some clay and make the first woman. Life was breathed into this creature and each goddess **bestowed** their own qualities upon her until she became a most **exquisite** being. She was named Pandora, meaning all-gifted woman, and Zeus sent her to Epimetheus.

He was lonely now that his brother had been banished from Olympus, so the gentle tapping at his door one day was a welcome surprise.

"What an amazing being!" he declared as he beheld Pandora's astonishing beauty.

When Pandora smiled it was as if warm sunbeams fell like golden liquid onto his skin.

"I am Pandora," she said. "Gift of the gods."

Even after Zeus' punishment of Prometheus, Epimetheus didn't think to mistrust Zeus' gift. Instead he said, "Truly the gods have smiled upon me. In your beauty lies the key to my joy!"

He wasted no time in asking her to be his wife.

Now, as well as her many qualities, Pandora brought with her a box, which Zeus commanded her never, ever to open. Epimetheus also urged Pandora to obey the gods and never open the mysterious casket.

"But husband," she said. "What if the contents of the box could make us even happier? Don't we deserve the greatest contentment?"

Still Epimetheus always resisted the temptation of agreeing to let his wife open the box.

"Let us be grateful for the life that we have," he pleaded. "There is nothing more we need."

But he knew that Pandora's heart was growing dark with longing to solve the mystery of the box.

⑧ One of the gifts bestowed upon Pandora was that of curiosity. She yearned and burned to know the secret of the box. Her inquisitiveness consumed her – it was stronger than her gift of obedience.

The box seemed like a powerful magnet drawing her closer to its secrets. One day, she waited until her husband was busy working outside. Kneeling beside it, she ran her trembling hands over its wooden lid. Pale fingers found the cold metal of the clasp. Just one flick to lift that clasp. A gentle lifting of the lid, not too wide, just enough to peep inside and satisfy the terrible hunger to solve the mystery.

As if to guide her faltering hand and heart, from within the chest came the sound of many voices, singing in harmonies that were enchanting and yet full of sorrow. She felt her heart swell and surge as they sang the same phrase over and over again.

"Release us from our ceaseless toil... release us from our ceaseless toil... release us from our ceaseless toil..."

Unable to resist, Pandora released the clasp and lifted the heavy lid...

In an instant, that was to change life on earth forever, the heavenly voices Pandora had heard became hideous shrieks; the sunlit room she was in was engulfed in darkness as black as the deepest well and a million winged creatures, spitting hatred and scattering all the evils of the world, flew out of Pandora's box.

Distraught, she fell upon it pressing down on the lid to stop the evil beings. But it was too late. Released by the power of Pandora's curiosity, they had escaped their prison. Never again would mankind be free of the evils of sickness, poverty, pain, envy, hunger and everything that leads to human despair. Zeus had indeed wounded all humanity for all eternity.

Only one winged creature was left in the box, and that was Hope. Even the gods who helped Zeus to punish mankind knew that Hope was needed in the face of so much evil in the world. That is why Hope abides in all our hearts whenever she is needed to save us from despair.

How to Write Instructions

1. First, find something useful to write instructions for: cooking a meal, building a model, using an mp3 player are possibilities. 'How to make your teacher's desk explode' certainly sounds both useful and fun, but probably won't go down very well.

2. Next, make a list of the things that you need. It would be rather inconvenient if you got halfway through trying to build a table and then realised you didn't have a hammer, a saw...or wood.

3. Use plenty of imperative verbs, especially at the start of sentences. Teachers like these because they're words that tell you what to do: *be quiet, sit down, stop picking your nose*, etc. Recipes use words such as *add, mix, stir*, etc.

4. Try to begin some instructions with an adverb. This will get you mega brownie points, as teachers love adverbs even more than tea and biscuits!

5. Make sure your instructions are in the right sequence. It's no use telling someone to "serve with salad" and then "whisk the eggs and add to the bowl". Not unless you want to poison them.

6. Next, place numbers or bullet points at the start of each instruction. Numbers usually work best, as they show which order to do things in. It's traditional to start with 1 for the first instruction, rather than 239½.

7. Finally, add diagrams or photos. Some people find pictures easier to follow than sentences on their own. Try to include photos that show the reader what to do, rather than photos of your favourite football team, your holiday in Spain, etc.

How to Write a Greek Myth

1. First, choose your hero carefully. Suitable names might be 'Hercules', 'Perseus', or 'Prometheus'. 'Baz' is not suitable. If in doubt, go for a name with '-us' at the end. No, not 'Bazzus'.

2. Secondly, give him a seemingly impossible task, such as slaying whole armies with nothing more than a bent drinking straw.

3. Next, make up a reason why the gods have chosen to give him this task. He may have done something to upset them. No, "nicking Zeus' football boots" is not an acceptable reason.

4. After that, throw in a creature with magical powers who'll try to prevent him from achieving his task. It helps if this creature has more or less of a particular body part than it should have, e.g. six heads, one eye, thirty-seven legs, each with nine razor-sharp claws.

5. Add a female love interest (optional). Usually she will get in the way and distract him, with fatal or near-fatal consequences. (No offence girls, that's just the way it is in myth world.)

6. Finally, find a way to make your hero triumph. He will overcome all obstacles, against all odds, succeed in his quest and be rewarded with great riches. Or...

7. Find a way to make your hero fail valiantly. He'll come within a whisker of success, only to fail because he can't fly, can't resist females (see 5 above), can't see that a bent drinking straw is no weapon with which to confront a whole army of foes, etc.

Have a Go at...
Chocolate Chip Ice Cream!

Legend has it that the Roman Emperor Nero had snow and ice brought down from the mountains and mixed with honey, fruit and nectar – just for him, of course! The first records of *milk-based* ice cream in Europe date from the seventeenth century.

Why not try making some yourself? No electric ice cream maker? No problem! Here's how to make super-smooth ice cream by hand.

Good cooks gather all their ingredients together before they begin. You'll need:

500ml milk
2 eggs, beaten
¼ tsp salt
nutmeg
500ml whipping cream
300g sugar
½ tsp vanilla extract
200g packet of chocolate chip

1. First, combine the milk, eggs, cream, sugar and salt in a large saucepan. Heat it slowly, stirring continuously with a whisk to prevent lumps.
Warning: If you're using a non-stick pan, use a plastic whisk, not a metal one!

2. When the mixture thickens, remove from the heat. Test it by stirring with a wooden spoon, then lifting the spoon out. If the mixture coats the spoon without running off, it's ready.

3. Pour your mixture into a glass bowl (or plastic if you prefer) and leave to cool. This may take up to two hours.

Safety first...

Remember to get a grown-up to help you!

4. When it has cooled, stir in the vanilla extract, chocolate chips and a pinch of nutmeg. Or you could try mashed strawberries, bananas or pistachio nuts!

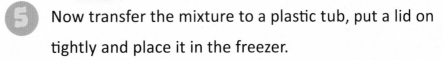

5. Now transfer the mixture to a plastic tub, put a lid on tightly and place it in the freezer.

6. Check your ice cream after half an hour. As soon as it sets at the edges, take it out of the freezer, tip it back into the glass bowl and beat it thoroughly with a wooden spoon. This keeps it smooth. Next, put it back into the tub and return to the freezer.

7. Repeat the beating process for a super-smooth result.

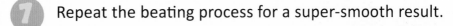

8. Remember to take the ice cream out of the freezer half an hour before you want to eat it, to soften it slightly. Finally, squirt on a sauce of your choice and…enjoy!

Bling!

Jon Blake

This is a story passed on to me by a tiny magical being, of which you will hear more soon.

It's a hard world. Everyone knows that. There are winners and there are losers. The winners are on telly 24/7, bragging about their cribs, their wheels, their bling. They like to tell us what great people they are, people who do stuff for charity, people who care about the losers, as long as the losers don't try to climb their garden wall or start a revolution.

The winners like to say that anyone can make it, because they made it. But most people never do make it. Most people are losers.

At least, that's how Billy Midas saw things. Even at age 10, Billy was quite sure he was a loser. His parents were divorced, he didn't live in a mansion, and his trainers were spelt 'Adadas' because they were fakes from Splott Market.

Billy possessed only one thing which was beautiful, and strictly speaking, he didn't even own that. Goji was his cat, a lean fishbone tabby so perfectly marked she was a natural miracle. Whenever Billy had a bad day at school, there was always Goji to climb on to his shoulder and purr sweet nothings into his ear. No matter how dismal the yard looked, no matter how drab the kitchen was, there was always Goji to brighten it up, to give it warmth, to make it home.

Billy loved Goji. Goji was his constant companion. It was Goji who helped Billy find the Chimichanga.

At first Billy thought Goji had found a mouse. She was crouched dead still in the yard, between an old bike wheel and a broken toy oven, eyes fixed on the hedge. As Billy got nearer he heard movements among the leaves, then spotted something hopping about, frantic and afraid.

It wasn't a mouse. It wasn't a bird either. It was some kind of person, a tiny person, with his leg caught in a length of garden twine.

"It's OK," said Billy. He shooed Goji away and reached in to free the tiny being. The being seemed to sense immediately that Billy was a friend, and stayed quite still as Billy picked away the twine.

"What are you?" asked Billy.

"A Chimichanga," replied the being.

"What's a Chimichanga?" asked Billy.

"A thingummyjig," replied the being.

Billy viewed the little creature doubtfully. Billy wasn't the kind of boy to believe in pixies, wood nymphs, ghosts, or anything with a name he hadn't heard of.

"As you've saved my life," continued the Chimichanga, "I shall grant you a wish."

Billy was still doubtful. Billy was a loser, and nothing good ever happened to losers.

"What kind of wish?" he asked.

"What do you most want?" asked the Chimichanga.

"Gold," replied Billy.

The Chimichanga closed his eyes and concentrated for a few moments.

"Where is your room?" he asked.

"Up there on the left," replied Billy.

The Chimichanga concentrated a few seconds longer.

"Go up there now," he declared. "You will find a golden cushion. Place anything of your choice on that cushion, wait one hour, and you will find it turned to gold."

"I'll believe that when I see it," replied Billy.

"Of course," said the Chimichanga. "If you ever need me again, just call."

With that, twin casings on the creature's back split apart, buzzing wings burst out, and the Chimichanga was gone on the wind.

Billy hurried to his bedroom. Just as promised, a cushion lay on the floor, though there was nothing very special-looking about it, apart from the fact it was golden.

"We'll see about this!" declared Billy. He took off the name bracelet he'd bought for a fiver at Splott Market, laid it on the cushion, and not expecting much, went off to play with Goji.

One hour later Billy was back. The Chimichanga had been as good as his word.

Billy's trashy old chrome bracelet now **glinted with the heavenly glow of gold** – and by the look of it, gold of the highest purity.

Billy slipped the bracelet onto his wrist. It was **heavy with luxury**. Billy turned his wrist, letting it fall softly one way then the other, hardly aware that Goji was rubbing round his ankles in the hope of tea.

"Now let's see who ignores me," he murmured.

The next day, Billy strolled into school as cool as a cucumber. He scanned the playground and picked out Calum and Ed. Calum and Ed were top dogs in Year 6, kids everyone listened to, kids who never had the time of day for a worm like Billy.

Billy sauntered over. As he passed Calum and Ed he raised his **glittering wrist** and waved.

"Hi, guys," he said. Calum's eyes practically popped.

19

"What's that on your wrist?" he demanded.

Billy was quickly surrounded.

"What's the matter?" asked Billy. "Never seen twenty-four carat gold before?"

"Where d'you get it?" demanded Ed.

"Wouldn't you like to know?" replied Billy.

All that day, Billy's name bracelet was the talk of the school. Some people thought he must have come into money. Others thought he'd stolen the bracelet. Billy admitted nothing and denied nothing. He was quietly relishing being the centre of attention.

Come afternoon break, interest was dwindling. It was time to create a new stir.

"Does anyone else want some gold?" he asked.

There was no shortage of takers. Billy picked out Calum.

"Give us your silver chain," he said, "and I'll bring it back pure gold."

Calum fingered the chain that hung around his neck. It had been a present from his grandad. The chain was worth a few quid, but that was nothing compared to what it would be worth if Billy kept his word.

"You better look after it," said Calum.

"No worries," replied Billy.

Calum removed the chain and handed it to Billy.

"Now," said Billy. "What's in it for me?"

"If you can turn this chain into gold," replied Calum. "You'll be my friend for life."

Goji was mewing loudly when Billy got home. Goji liked to sleep on Billy's bed and couldn't understand why the bedroom door was closed. But Billy had to be ultra-careful now he'd got the golden cushion. He didn't want his little sister pulling it apart or his mum putting it in the washing machine.

Billy fed Goji, gave her a brief tickle, then got down to the important business. If he could make Calum his friend the rest would surely follow.

That evening the cushion worked its magic just as surely as before, and the next day Billy strolled into school with the perfect prize in his pocket. As soon as he set eyes on the chain, Calum greedily seized it, checking it over for familiar marks.

"Awesome!" he said. "How did you do this?"

Billy tapped his nose.

"You're a mate, Billy," said Calum.

Billy raised his palm. Calum high-fived it. A **glow of satisfaction** spread through Billy, until he was sure his whole being must be **gleaming like gold**.

"Can you do my earring?" asked Ed.

"Sorted," replied Billy.

Soon half of Billy's classmates were wearing gold. Some teachers were asking questions and no doubt some parents as well. That didn't bother Billy. Billy was king of the hill now, cock of the walk, top of the tree. He walked with a slow swagger and a poker face, because top dogs didn't need to smile. Most boys high-fived him everywhere he went and some girls followed him around. There were those who didn't care for the way he'd changed, but what did that matter to Billy? The people who didn't like him were losers, and he'd started to despise losers. Then again, he'd started to despise some of his new friends as well. It was so easy to make them sit up and beg, like faithful puppydogs. Billy thought maybe he'd bring in some gold dog-collars and see if they'd faithfully wear them. But he decided to make himself a third neck chain instead.

Then Billy got jumped on his way home from school. Three boys, big boys. Billy wasn't hurt, but two of his chains and his name bracelet were snatched.

"You OK, Billy?" asked Ed, arriving on the scene.

"Those boys are dead," said Billy. His voice quavered.

"You need to protect yourself," said Ed.

"What I need," said Billy, "is bodyguards."

From that day on, Billy was never seen without the two hardest boys in school.

The two chains and name bracelet were easily replaced, and

Billy began to think about turning bigger things to gold, and turning that gold into money. Every door was open to him now, even though every door had to be locked and bolted as soon as he was inside it.

Then, one day, Billy came home to an eerie silence. Normally Goji was quick to greet him, either with a quick tour of his legs or a loud miaow from wherever she was curled up. Billy called her, but there was no reply.

Billy checked all the downstairs rooms, then went up to his bedroom. To his alarm, he saw that the door was a few centimetres open.

Surely he'd locked it that morning?

Anxiously, Billy pressed the door open. His eyes immediately went to the top of the wardrobe where he normally stored the cushion. It wasn't there.

With mounting fear, Billy now turned his attention to the desk where he'd last used the cushion. To his utter horror, he saw that the cushion was still there, and upon it the stock-still body of a cat, **gleaming with the terrible beauty** of twenty-four carat gold.

Billy moved forward into the room. It was as if he was on automatic pilot, no longer in control of his own actions. Every detail of his precious cat was preserved – every whisker, every claw, every tiny hair. If Billy had not been in such a state of shock he might have seen it as a beautiful work of art.

Billy laid a trembling hand on Goji's side. She was cold as stone.

"You stupid cat!" he whimpered.

But Billy knew it was he who was stupid. Billy had left the cushion out and the door open. Billy had asked for the cushion in the first place.

Billy picked up Goji. In place of a living, purring cat there was nothing but heavy metal and a fixed, unseeing stare.

Feeling her dead weight, Billy let out a howl. He had to do something!

Billy ran out into the back yard, still with the golden cat in his arms.

"Chimichanga!" he cried. It was a cry loud enough to wake the dead – or so the saying goes. Nothing.

"Chimichanga!" he cried again. "Help me!"

There was a stirring in the bushes, a faint glow, and then, to Billy's relief, the tiny being emerged.

Billy held out the golden cat towards it. "Bring her back!" he cried.

"You wanted gold," said the Chimichanga.

"Yes, but not my cat!" pleaded Billy. "Can you bring her back?"

The Chimichanga considered. "It is possible," he said.

"Then do it!" cried Billy.

"It's not as simple as that," replied the Chimichanga.

"Why not?" pleaded Billy.

"If I reverse the power of the gold-maker," replied the Chimichanga, "it will be reversed forever."

"I don't care!" cried Billy.

"And everything that was made gold," continued the Chimichanga, "will return to its former state."

Billy was paralysed. Lose all his gold? Lose all the gold he'd given his new friends? Lose the glittering future he'd mapped out for himself?

Billy thought of the big shots he'd seen on the telly. Those people made it because they let nothing stand in their way. Those people would laugh at the idea of giving it all up for a cat. That was what made them the kind of people they were.

Then Billy looked down again at Goji, her life in his hands. He imagined the emptiness of a world without her.

"I can't stay," said the Chimichanga. "You must decide."

Billy took a deep breath. He felt as if the weight of the whole world was on his shoulders.

"Promise you'll never tell anyone what I say next," he said.

"I promise," replied the Chimichanga.

Once again, the Chimichanga was as good as his word.

The end

Bravery Award fo Fire Hero Boy

A **TEENAGE HERO** who saved a young family from a burning house has been recommended for a bravery award by his local fire service.

Keen sportsman Conor McGrath, 14, took a dramatic and dangerous rescue bid in his stride when he caught two children dropped from the first floor of their flame-engulfed home last week.

Conor and his father, Shaun McGrath

The teenager, a sturdy 6ft 1in and 14 stone, persuaded their terrified mother to throw daughter Koli, aged five, and son Callan, aged 13, to safety, promising to catch them from where he stood 10 feet below.

And true to his promise Conor – whose proud father Shaun McGrath was also on hand to catch mother Lindsay McGuinness as she followed her children out of the already blown out window – made a clean catch, which saw both children shaken but uninjured following their harrowing ordeal.

Of his fearless rescue Conor said: "It was one of those things that you don't think about – you just act.

"I saw the mother and children at the window and it was like a reflex action. When you need to get people to safety, it takes no thinking about."

The brave youngster, hailed as a hero by family, friends and neighbours alike, added: "When you think about it after, it seems scarier than it was at the time.

"It was only a freefall of about three feet for them really and I alway

...he house, after the fire.

...new I would catch them – I had no ...her choice."

...Conor's father Shaun, whose father ...ils from Cork City, was also at the ...ene in Green Lane, close to their ...ome in Charlesworth Avenue, Bolton, ... around 7pm.

...He explained: "We had just ...ome back from a jog and were only ... the first door when my wife went ...nning into the back garden – ...e thought something had hit our ...ighbour's roof.

"Initially, because of the loudness ... the bang, we thought something ...d literally dropped out of the sky.

"So we ran round to the front and ...uld see our neighbour and her two children trapped in the top floor front bedroom of the house – they were screaming and shouting and it was all pretty smoky."

Shaun added: "It was quite a terrifying thing to see as the gas explosion had blown out all the front windows of the house.

"I got in through one of the smashed windows and tried to get up to the family, but the stairs were a ball of flames so I had to come back out.

"In the meantime my son told the mother to throw the two children out of the window for him to catch. I am of course very proud of Conor, he is a calm lad and did what he felt was right."

Conor has now been recommended for a bravery award by Bolton's Deputy Borough Commander, Ian Bailey.

He said: "We will be looking into the full details of the incident and a decision will be made on what award Conor will receive.

"With the situation he was faced with it is almost incomprehensible that a 14-year-old lad can act in such a calm and composed manner."

Reproduced from *The Irish Post*

NEWSHOUND

Home

World News

UK News

Sport

Animal Kingdom

Entertainment

Music

Celeb-watch

Games

Contact Us

Sherlock's Paws for Thought

Your chance to give your opinion on one of today's burning topics:

Should exotic birds be kept as caged pets?

Join our chat forum by clicking <u>here</u>.

Ape escape put on hold

Scientists tell us that human and apes have much in common. One Sydney Zoo primate seems to have more in common than most.

Karta, a 27-year-old orang-utan, had clearly had her fill of life behind bars. In a dare-devil plan, she uprooted a tree and used it to batter down the electrified fence of her enclosure. Only one more barrier remained between ape and freedom: the outer wall. Piling up rubbish in a heap against the wall, she prepared to make her escape into the Australian streets. Roaming, climbing, running free...

But then Karta showed us the even more human side to her character. One eyewitness, 10-year-old Simon Evans, reported: "She was about to clamber on top of the rubbish to get over the wall, but then she just stopped and sat down. It looked like she was thinking things through, wondering if it was really worth all the effort. Then she turned round and made her way back to her cage."

Keepers at the zoo described Karta as "highly intelligent". Karta herself was unavailable for comment. Maybe she was revising for her driving test!

▶ <u>More stories like this</u>

atest: Education Department set to scrap homework for primary school children.

oggers in
oon Match Bid

d Cheeseman,
airman of Clapham
oggers football
ub, revealed that
e club were in talks

th US space agency NASA in a bid to stage the
st football match on the Moon, scheduled to be
ayed next... ▶ **Full story**

ational Gallery holds
t painting exhibition

what is believed to be a world first, London is
host an exhibition of paintings by a cat! The
2 purrfect canvases, on subjects including birds
nd mice, represent the life's work of Cardiff
bby, Cruncher, who apparently dips her paws
paint before carefully... ▶ **Full story**

nimal Archive

Uhu the
verweight
tick insect.

Missing rabbit
turns up on
Brazilian beach.

Bus-driving
camel causes
Cairo chaos.

Sniff it out!

Sherlock's top stories from
around the globe today:

World leaders in
climate change
meeting.

New planet
discovered?

Underwater
car tested in
Australia.

Ears Your Chance!

Fancy yourself as an artist?
Why not enter our illustration
competition!

Imagine the story behind the
headline below then draw an
illustration that could appear
alongside the article.

**Bathers left high and dry
as thirsty elephant empties
hotel pool!**

Email your piccy to us – just
follow the link below!

Email us

Beach Bonanza!

Container ship *MSC Napoli* was deliberately beached in Lyme Bay after it was damaged in storms on the way to South Africa in January 2007.

Thousands of people came to Branscombe beach to scavenge the contents of the 50 containers, which washed ashore.

Scavengers took goods washed up on the beach. There was everything from motorcycles to nappies!

In July 2007, the ship was split in two by controlled explosions.

Salvagers then worked for five months to remove the final remaining sections of the container ship.

Goodnight Stroud

The Clock Tower glowers.
Its hands fidget
towards dawn.

Dark streets yawn.
    It's late –
the streets wait –
    restless as rain.

Trains idle up sidelines;
a cyclist sidles by.

Black taxis scuttle
down back alleys.
A bright bus blunders
up the High Street.

The Belisha Beacon blinks.

Parked cars huddle,
like wet toads;
the night thinks
that the stars
are sending Morse code.

Pie Corbett

Last Night, I Saw The City Breathing

Last night, I saw the city breathing,
Great gusts of people,
Rushing in and
Puffing out
Of stations' singing mouths.

Last night, I saw the city laughing,
Takeaways got the giggles,
Cinemas split their sides,
And living rooms completely creased themselves!

Last night, I saw the city dancing.
Shadows were cheek to cheek with brick walls,
Trains wiggled their hips all over the place,
And the trees
in the breeze,
Put on a show for an audience of windows!

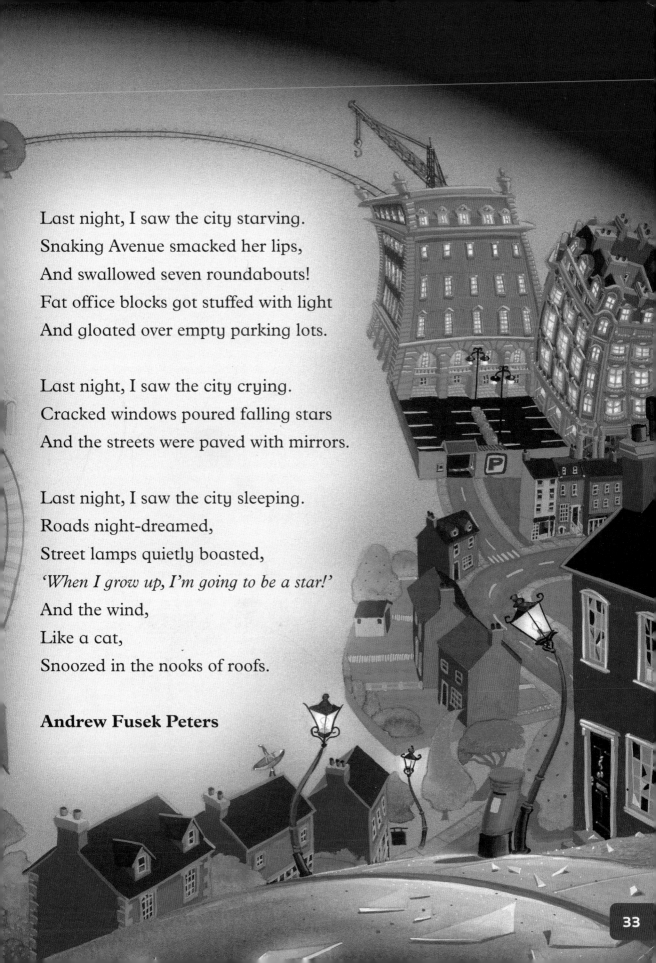

Last night, I saw the city starving.
Snaking Avenue smacked her lips,
And swallowed seven roundabouts!
Fat office blocks got stuffed with light
And gloated over empty parking lots.

Last night, I saw the city crying.
Cracked windows poured falling stars
And the streets were paved with mirrors.

Last night, I saw the city sleeping.
Roads night-dreamed,
Street lamps quietly boasted,
'When I grow up, I'm going to be a star!'
And the wind,
Like a cat,
Snoozed in the nooks of roofs.

Andrew Fusek Peters

MEET THE MONSTER!

FANS OF DENTON!

Are you planning to **stand and cheer** as our town centre is destroyed to put more money into the bottomless pockets of Denton United and their gang of solicitor friends?

Will you **support** the damage and disruption to your neighbourhoods as needless new roads and tramlines tear up the ground around your houses?

Will you **buy a ticket** to watch an area of outstanding beauty being dug up and concreted over so that a bunch of overpaid prima donnas can prance around kicking a football?

Perhaps you will **wave your banners and sing** as trees that have stood for thousands of years are uprooted and thousands of creatures are left without a home?

Surely not!

Then show your true support for Denton by attending the local residents' meeting at

**Denton Community Centre, Beech Avenue
Monday 22nd April at 7.30 p.m.**

DO YOUR BIT TO STOP THIS MONSTER FROM EATING UP OUR TOWN!

MEET THE FUTURE!

DENTON UNITED

Think Big Building Co.

Denton United is working with t[he] Think Big Building Co. and we are proud to unveil plans for the new **Winmore Football Stadium.**

The latest in glass and steel construction design, this superb 45,000 all-seater arena represents the ultimate in style and comfort for the twenty-first century football fan. United's supporters will soon enjoy unrestricted views, high-quality food and drink outlets and easy wheelchair access to all areas of the stadium. Just what you've been longing for!

No one wants to spend cold, damp afternoons shivering on those old terraces, do they? Our hi-tech retractable roof will make sure that everyone can sit snug and warm while they cheer United on to victory.

The town centre gets very busy on match days and Denton Park is under-used by the community, so our superb new stadium will be built on th[e] parkland outside the town. Our huge c[ar] park and new network of access roads will allow drivers to arrive and leave in record time. Of course we care deeply about the environment and so buses will run every ten minutes for those wh[o] prefer the greener option.

Denton's Youth Development programme will be the best in the country with a state-of-the-art training complex. Budding stars will have access to high levels of skills and fitnes[s] coaching, using possibly the finest equipment available to man. Adults joining the Winmore Leisure Club

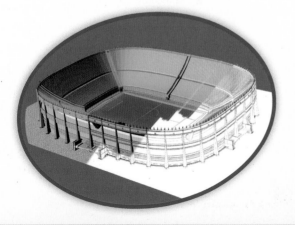

will be able to enjoy these luxurious facilities and can then relax afterwards in the swish surroundings of the café, bar and restaurant.

But the Winmore Stadium is not just about sport. There's much, much more...

The removable pitch means that the ultra-versatile stadium will become the most popular touring stop: pop stars, bands, comedians – they'll all be coming to Denton!

Not only that, the stadium will be a shopper's paradise! Our adjoining giant shopping mall will have outlets selling everything from newspapers to kitchens; from fun fashions to designer clothing.

Winmore! What more could you want?

Well, we've kept a total commitment to the community of Denton at the forefront of our minds. The stadium complex will bring thousands of much-needed jobs to the area. The events will attract huge numbers of people, resulting in a fantastic boost for local businesses. In fact, the Winmore Stadium will be like a mini city – a new Denton...

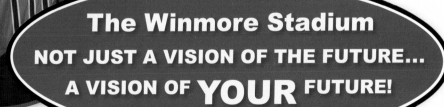

The Winmore Stadium
NOT JUST A VISION OF THE FUTURE...
A VISION OF **YOUR** FUTURE!

This Is NOT a Fairy Tale

Jeremy Strong

This is something that happened a long time ago before history began, before people knew what was real and what wasn't – although they *thought* they knew the difference. It was a time when bears and wolves **roamed** the countryside, when there were trolls and goblins, dwarves and unicorns, dragons and witches and wicked stepmothers and proud queens who were not as beautiful as Snow White, and so on… You get the picture.

* * *

Luke was a young man of eighteen. He was good-looking, but very poor. His father had died when a goat fell on him. (That was the sort of accidental death people had in those days. Luke's grandmother had been mown down by a flock of runaway chickens.) Luke was only six when his father died and after that he was brought up by his mother, Old Crone, and his pet dog, Shaggy.

There was little work to be found in the **ramshackle** village where Luke lived and because there was little work there was no money to be made. Luke made do as best he could.

He was happy to turn his hand to anything, so he did a bit of wood chopping here and a bit of shepherding there and so on. In this way he just about managed to keep himself fed, although his clothes would certainly not have won any fashion prizes. They were torn and tattered and dirty.

Luke did, however, have one big advantage despite his humble environment. He had a brain, and Luke's brain was a good brain and he used it for doing what brains do best of all – thinking. He used to listen to what all the wise old villagers used to chat about during the long dark evenings. He would lap up every word. He would listen to their old tales, **enthralled**.

The old villagers were very proud of their wisdom. They would sit round a winter fire and say things like: "We be wise old villagers. What I say is, before the last apple falls, there'll be trouble."

And all the other elders of the village would go: "Ooh, ahh, Old Jezebel, she be right there. Before the last apple falls, there'll be trouble!"

And then someone else might say: "Ah, but when the moon is red and the hawthorn is in bloom, that's the time to be darning socks!" And they would all nod their heads in agreement.

Luke would listen to all this ancient wisdom and he soon came to the conclusion that it was mostly a load of old nonsense. He worked out that if he lived his life based on the things the elders had told him he would never get anything done at all. He certainly was not going to wait for a red moon and blooming hawthorn before he set about darning *his* socks. He decided to use his own brain instead.

Now, it so happened that there was a lot of talk in the village about the local princess. Her name was Ramona and she lived at the top of the mountain. (The village was at the bottom.) It was said that Ramona had flaming-red hair and **was as beautiful as the sunset**. Very few people had actually seen the princess because she had never come down from the mountain, and they had never been up it.

The only way people knew about her was because occasionally messages were sent down from the castle. They were written on paper, folded into darts and **launched** over the battlements.

Ramona was due for marriage, but despite the best efforts of her parents, no suitable husband could be found. The rules for marriage were the usual weird rules that people used in those days. The prospective suitor had to climb the mountain from bottom to top and then he could claim the hand of the gorgeous Ramona. You may think there was little that was difficult about this, and you would be right to think that actually climbing the mountain – the climbing bit itself – was not terribly difficult.

No, the awkward bit was what might happen on the way. You see, as you went up the mountain you would quite likely meet with the Black Bear. If you didn't see *him* you would no doubt come across the Trolls of Tiddly Crag, or the Waggletooth Witch. Then there were the Wild Wolves of Black Fen, the Dragon of Doom and – most frightening of all – the Giant Man-Eating Unicorn That Nobody Had Ever Seen. So all the suitors died on their way up, and this was also why Ramona never came down from the castle and all the messages were sent down by paper dart. (You may wish to know how the villagers got messages up to the castle and the short answer is, they didn't. They had yet to invent a dart that could be flung that high.)

Now Luke was not only bright, he was adventurous. Nowadays he would have gone white-water rafting and bungee jumping, but nobody had heard of such things in those days, so he didn't. But he did want to see the world. He wanted to escape from the humdrum little village where half of the elders spouted nonsense. He wanted to travel, but he didn't want to do it by himself. He wanted a companion. So it was then that his thoughts turned towards the Princess Ramona.

Luke knew all about the dreadful creatures that haunted the mountain, yet he was still determined to see if he could win the hand of the beautiful Princess Ramona in marriage. He sat down and had a long, hard think. Then he got up and packed his bag. He put in some fruit, a sandwich and some chicken drumsticks for the journey,

because he didn't know how long it would take, and he set off up the mountain.

As he left the village the elders shouted after him: "If you see the Waggletooth Witch you must cross your fingers behind your back and run like the wind and shout out the alphabet backwards!"

Some of them offered this advice too: "When the Black Bear tries to eat you, rub your skin with acorn juice and hiss. Then the bear will vanish."

Even his mother had wise words for him: "Trolls love to dance. If you come across them you must play your magic violin and they will dance and dance until they drop down dead."

"Right," nodded Luke. He told everyone that he would certainly bear in mind their advice and he set off. He had not got far before he came across a patch of brambles as big as Europe. The brambles were thick and tall and covered in sharp, flesh-tearing thorns. What made them worse was that here and there he could see bits of torn clothing left behind by some of the princes who had tried to find a way through. There were even a few skeletons hanging around. They didn't look very happy.

Luke looked at the brambles and he thought for a bit and then he made himself a small fire. He found two nice bits of thick wood and pushed their ends into the fire and waited until they had caught the flame nicely. Armed with these **flaming brands** Luke advanced on the brambles. They sizzled and hissed and spat and curled up and shrivelled at the heat from the flames and so, bit by bit, Luke made his way through the brambles, leaving a nice, clean, charred path behind him, ready for his return.

Luke pressed on up the mountain, whistling. All of a sudden out popped the Waggletooth Witch. She was hairy, she was horrid. She was the ugliest thing Luke had ever laid eyes on. Her nose was like a giant parrot's beak, but covered with warts and pimples and sprouting hairs. Did Luke cross his fingers behind his back and run away saying the alphabet backwards? No.

"I'm going to put a nasty spell on you!" cackled the witch.

"Why's that?" asked Luke, quite reasonably.

"Because I'm so hideous and you are so handsome I cannot bear the sight of you." And the witch reached into her handbag and pulled out her wicked witch's wand.

"I don't know why you say you are hideous," said Luke, calmly. "I think you are extraordinary."

The witch, who was just in the process of making all the right sort of wavy movements with her wand before casting her spell, stopped in mid-wave. "What? Why do you say that?"

Luke boldly stepped forward. He didn't want to show how frightened he was. "Oh yes, you really are quite extraordinary. I have never seen a nose like yours. It is unique. It is wonderful!"

The Waggletooth Witch blushed. She did! She turned pink and then red and then back to pink. She fluttered her eyelashes. "Oh you! You're just saying that!"

(Luke was thinking: *Of course I'm saying that. You couldn't hear me if I weren't.* But he kept his thoughts to himself, which is always a wise thing to do at times such as this.)

"It's true," said Luke.

"Ah, well I am not sure I believe you," said the Waggletooth Witch with a cunning leer. "I bet you wouldn't dare kiss me."

Luke smiled. (Behind the smile his teeth were firmly gritted.) "I thought you'd never ask," he said, and he gave the witch a stonking kiss.

To say that the Waggletooth Witch was amazed would be an understatement. She staggered back, quite delighted. Nobody had ever kissed her before, not even her own mother when she was a child. "What a perfect gentleman you are. Nobody had ever done that to me. I wish you luck on your journey."

And Luke carried on up the mountain, thinking that a little kindness often went a long way. All at once the bushes parted and out sprang the Black Bear. Did Luke rub himself with acorn juice and hiss? No, he didn't.

"Grrrr," said the bear, in a bearish sort of way. "What are you doing halfway up this mountain?"

"I have come to seek the hand of the Princess Ramona," explained Luke.

"Oh really? Do you know how many princes I have eaten?"

"No, I don't," Luke answered truthfully.

"Thirty-two," said the bear, also truthfully.

"Then you must have been very hungry," Luke replied, and that stopped the bear in his tracks. The bear had never heard the like. Of course he had been hungry. That was why he ate all the princes.

Luke sat down at the bear's feet and patted the grass beside him. "In my bag I have some chicken. Would you like some?"

"What is chicken?" asked the bear, sitting down and gazing at Luke with great curiosity.

Luke got out the biggest chicken drumstick and he let the bear smell it. Then he gave it to the bear. The Black Bear ate the chicken and licked his lips and said he thought that chicken drumstick was a lot nicer than princes and a lot less bony.

Then he wished Luke good luck with his journey and hoped that they would meet again.

Luke carried on up the mountain and before long he came face to face with the Trolls of Tiddly Crag. *What a busy day I'm having*, thought Luke. The trolls surrounded Luke and danced round him chanting horrible things. They were short, ugly little creatures, with needle-sharp teeth and a taste for human flesh. Now they bared their teeth and pulled horrible faces at Luke.

Did Luke pull out his magic violin and make them dance until they all dropped down dead? Of course not. He didn't have a magic violin and he didn't know how to play the violin even if he *did* have one.

Instead he just stood there and laughed. "You're so cute!" he told the trolls.

"No we're not. We're horrible!" yelled the Chief Troll.

"But you're so cuddly," insisted Luke, giving them a great big smile.

"Shut up!" roared the Chief Troll. "We're horrible, horrible, horrible!"

Luke shook his head and repeated quietly, "Cute!"

"Aargh!" screamed the Chief Troll. "We are horrible!" and he flew into such a rage that he exploded on the spot. BANG! The other trolls ran away.

Soon after this, Luke reached the top of the mountain and he walked into the castle and found the Princess Ramona, who was every bit as beautiful as everyone had said.

"Great heavens above," cried Ramona, "someone has actually made it to the top of the mountain and he's rather gorgeous – despite the totally untrendy clothes and strong smell of garlic."

For the sake of decency and so on I am going to leave out the bit where they fall in love and have a smooch, but they did all that and then Luke said it was time to go back down the mountain.

"But I can't," said Ramona. "There's a witch down there, and a bear and trolls and all sorts of horrible creatures and brambles and I might tear my dress."

"We can't stay up here for ever," said Luke. "Down there, at the bottom of the mountain, that is where the rest of the world starts and there is so much to see and to do and I am going to see it and do it and I want you to be with me."

"I dearly want to see the rest of the world," murmured Ramona.

"And I want to be with you more than anything else."

But Ramona was very frightened and she would not go down the mountain. Luke eventually set off on his own. "I shall wait for one day," he told her. "After that I shall set off on my own if you have not arrived. You must make up your mind Ramona. You must **overcome** your own fear. I cannot do that for you."

Halfway down the mountain Luke met the trolls again. "Cute," he smiled and this time they hid under rocks before any more of them could explode. He met the Black Bear but the chicken was finished so he gave the bear a salad sandwich instead.

"Hmmm, nice," said the bear. "People often forget that bears are omnivores. I love eating greens."

Next up was the Waggletooth Witch, who simply blushed and smiled and fluttered her eyelashes. Luke got away with blowing her a kiss and after that he reached the bottom of the mountain without any further problems. He never did see the Giant Man-Eating Unicorn That Nobody Had Ever Seen, which didn't surprise Luke but did surprise all the villagers when they asked what had happened.

Meanwhile, on top of the mountain, Ramona gazed back down towards the village. And she wondered. *Did she dare?* She desperately wanted to be with Luke and to explore the world and escape from her horrible castle.

But – was her love strong enough to overcome her fears?

And – if she did overcome her fears and she set off down the mountain, how would she deal with the Waggletooth Witch and the trolls and the bear and the brambles? Would she be as wise and kind as Luke?

You see, this story does not have a fairy-tale ending, because it isn't a fairy tale. In real life there are always problems, and *you* have to solve them.

The End

Epilogue

Why isn't this a fairy tale? Because it hasn't got any fairies in it. In fact, do you know ANY fairy tales that HAVE got fairies in them?

Biography
JEREMY STRONG

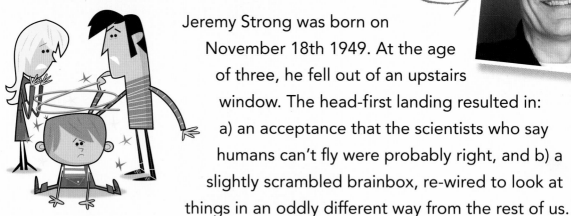

Jeremy Strong was born on November 18th 1949. At the age of three, he fell out of an upstairs window. The head-first landing resulted in: a) an acceptance that the scientists who say humans can't fly were probably right, and b) a slightly scrambled brainbox, re-wired to look at things in an oddly different way from the rest of us.

His mother, a teacher, was from Northern Rhodesia (now called Zambia), and her stories of life in the wilderness, full of lions and deadly snakes, fed his imagination. He inherited his writing skills from his father, who, although he was a chemist, had also written three novels. With his sister and two brothers he grew up (quarrelling, as you do) in a house on the outskirts of London. The garden backed onto fields, so his free time was spent playing and exploring in the wild outdoors. As a result he was happy, healthy, and generally suffering from some kind of injury or other – scratches from branches and scuffles, and bruises from falling out of trees. He enjoyed reading, particularly Rudyard Kipling's *Just So Stories*. No comics or pop music were allowed at home – so at school he would keenly read any comics his friends had.

Timeline:

1949 Born in Eltham, South-East London

1954–1968 Educated at Wyborne Primary School then Haberdashers' Aske's, both in London

1969–1972 Studied English at York University

1973 Trained to be a teacher at College of Ripon and St John, York

Beginnings

Jeremy was successful in only four areas of school life: playtimes, lunchtimes, going home...and writing stories. He was fortunate in having a teacher in Years 3 and 4 who not only encouraged him to write, but also told him that his stories were very good. Looking at the shelves of books in his local library, he dreamt that one day somebody would pull one of his books down from the shelf and actually enjoy reading it.

Development

After leaving school Jeremy went to university to study English, and got a job in a bakery, stuffing jam into doughnuts. When not at work he was writing stories, perfecting his craft. Training as a teacher, he took a job in a primary school, and moved away from writing for adults to concentrate on books for children.

The finished article

Over the years Jeremy climbed his way up the teaching tree to the giddy heights of Headmaster, writing in his spare time. By 1991 his books were successful enough for him to become a full-time writer. Since then he has averaged three or four books every year, and his total is currently over seventy. His home today is in Bradford-on-Avon near Bath, and when not writing he spends his days visiting schools, looking to inspire new young writers. He lives with his second wife Gillie, her two children and his cat Jeeves.

1974–1991 Taught at various schools in the south of England

1978 Published first book, *Smith's Tale*

1997 *The Hundred-Mile-An-Hour Dog* won Children's Book of the Year Award

Jeremy Strong's books have won many awards:

1997   *The Hundred-Mile-An-Hour Dog* won the Children's Book of the Year Award.

2004   *My Granny's Great Escape* won the Prix Chronos Award.

2006   *Stuff* won the Manchester Book Award.

2008   *Beware! Killer Tomatoes* won both the Sheffield and Leicester Book Awards.

Autobiography
My (Not So Serious) Story *by Jeremy Strong*

Children often ask me why my books are always 'funny'. I suppose my sense of humour has always been a bit wacky. As a child I loved Spike Milligan's daft poetry, and I like to think that some of that surreal daftness comes through in my books. Maybe it was the bang on my head when I fell out of the window, but my imagination has always been rather odd. I remember not wanting to throw a sweet wrapper into an empty bin because I thought it might feel lonely in there on its own. I ended up tearing it in half so that each piece would have a friend to talk to. Bizarre? Yes, I suppose it is.

I have tried to write serious books. In fact my Viking books were originally intended to be the gruesome adventures of a quite vicious character. The problem was that I didn't really enjoy the brutality of

it all, so I started to add funny bits to lighten it up. Before I knew it he'd turned into a rather lovable, cuddly, comic Viking.

My brain is always ready, waiting for the next idea to hatch. It might be something I see or hear on the street, or even a dream. Wherever I go I carry a notebook so that I can jot down ideas. Some of them never come to anything, and some may stay as notes for years before I come back to them. Once my mind gets to work on a new story I have to spend weeks writing down ideas, fleshing out my characters, deciding how the plot line will go, sorting out problems, and generally staring out of the window while the brain cogs slowly turn.

After all that planning, the writing's the easiest part. Mind you I don't always get it right first time. One of my favourites, *The Hundred-Mile-An-Hour Dog*, had to be written three times before my publisher was happy – it took me the first two goes to realise that it would be much better written in the first person, through the eyes of Streaker's owner, Trevor. Which shows you're never too old to learn!

Most of my writing is done in my garden 'shed' (it's actually quite grand, with a huge desk and even a fridge), under the watchful eye of Jeeves. Like any other writer though, I never know when my mind is going to start churning words out, so I also write 'on the move', wherever I happen to be.

Biography
Anthony Horowitz

THE BOY:

Born: April 5th 1955 in Stanmore, England (at the northern edge of London).

Family: A middle child with an older brother and younger sister. Father worked as a solicitor but he was very mysterious and never talked about his work. Much closer to his mother who introduced him to books and used to read horror stories to him at night. Had a 'truly evil' grandmother (Anthony's words)!

Lifestyle: Big house, lots of nannies, gardeners, butlers but not much fun. Packed off to boarding school ASAP. The *Tintin* adventure books inspired him to become a writer. Loved spy adventures, especially James Bond.

Education: Orley Farm boarding school (boys only) from age 8. Nightmare of a place with vicious staff and a brutal Headmaster. Used stories as a way of escape…telling stories to entertain the other boys. Moved on to happier times at Rugb School and the University of York.

THE MAN:

Career: Knew he wanted to be a writer from age 8. First book to be published was *Sinister Secret of Frederick K Bower* in 1979 at age 23. Researches thoroughly before writing, travelling to places where books set, trying to experience at first hand what characters experien in books. People from life often appear as characters in his books (yes, including that Headmaster).

TIMELINE:

1955 Born April 5th, London   **1963** Sent to Orley Farm boarding school   **1979** First book published   **1988** Got ma in Hong Kong

Family: Married Jill Green in 1988, in Hong Kong. Ceremony in Chinese so didn't understand a word! Two sons: Nicholas Mark (b. 1989), Cassian James (b. 1991).

Hobbies: Travel, scuba diving, going to cinema (fav. film *The Third Man* spy adventure).

Pets: Chocolate Labrador, "Lucky". Run over twice, so probably not!

THE BOOKS:

Major breakthrough: *The Diamond Brothers* series, heroes Nick and Tim. *The Falcon's Malteser* was turned into a film (*Just Ask for Diamond*).

Most famous for: Teen spy adventure series about 14-year-old spy Alex Rider, who works undercover for MI6. 12 million copies sold worldwide. Also hit TV drama series, *Foyle's War*.

Awards: Red House Children's Book Award, 2003, for *Skeleton Key*. The Lew Grade Audience Award at the BAFTA Television Awards for *Foyle's War* in 2003.

British Book Awards – Children's Book of the Year for *Ark Angel*, 2006. In 2008, Anthony made the National Year of Reading's first Champion Author.

Also written: 22 two-hour films for *Foyle's War*! Plus *Collision*, *Midsomer Murders*, and *Poirot*. Feature films – *The Gathering* (horror) and *Stormbreaker*.

2000 First Alex Rider novel, *Stormbreaker*, published

2006 *Stormbreaker* feature film released

2009 *Crocodile Tears* published, (*Alex Rider* series book 8)

Dragon Slayer

Gill Howell

The tiny village of Yishan nestled deep in a valley close to the foothills of an **ancient extinct** volcano. The volcano hadn't erupted for centuries so the villagers dwelt there contentedly in their wooded valley. It was customary for villages in China to have an Elder or Wise Man as the head of the village and Yishan was no exception. The villagers took their problems to the Elder who sorted out any troubles or disputes. In rare times of drought or flood, he was the one who drew up a plan of action and organised the villagers. If strangers threatened their way of life, he would drive them away and keep the village safe. So when a great emerald-green dragon made his home on the topmost rim of the volcano, it was to the Wise Man, Yen, that the villagers turned.

He pondered the problem for two days and then went to the ancient ceremonial bell at the centre of the village. Taking up a hammer, Yen struck it once and the tone rang out through the village and fields to call a meeting of all the villagers. They crowded into the meeting hall where Yen stood.

"We do not need to fear this dragon," he said and stroked his long grey beard from chin to tip.

"There is nothing here for him. We have no gold
or jewels and everyone knows that these are what
dragons desire most. He will soon be gone."

And so the people were comforted and went about
their daily lives. But then one day a great beating
sound was heard and the village **darkened beneath
the shadow** of the dragon's enormous scaly wings as he flew over it. The
people cowered in fear as they watched him circle overhead. Then, with
a final roar of red and orange flames, he was gone.

"He has gone!" called Yen triumphantly. "I told you we had nothing
to fear!"

"Thank you, Yen," said all the villagers, "you are such a wise village
Elder!" and the people continued with their everyday lives once more.

But then the dragon came in the night and stole a goat. And again
and again he came back. At first he took small animals, goats and dogs,
but then grew bolder, swooping down even in the day time to pluck their
animals from the midst of the village. More and more disappeared and the
people complained loudly.

"We are losing our livestock, Yen," they told the Elder. "Soon we will
have nothing left to eat."

Yen pondered the problem for a day and called the villagers to another
meeting. He stood before them, stroking his long grey beard.

"This dragon will soon tire of our animals. We should do nothing to
provoke him and then he will go away," said Yen.

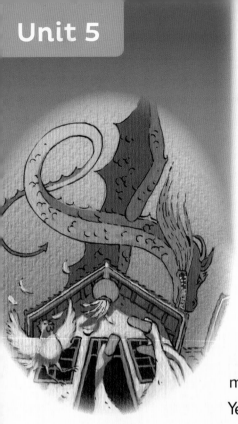

The villagers muttered amongst themselves but agreed that Yen was probably right, and so nothing was done to hinder the dragon's raids on their village.

Then one dreadful day, a child disappeared. At first, the child's mother searched the village but with no success. She grew increasingly distressed and called on Yen.

"My youngest son, Lin, has disappeared," she sobbed. "I have searched the whole village but no one has seen him since morning. Please help me, Yen!"

Yen organised a search party. They searched the village once more as the women wrung their hands and watched anxiously. They then searched the wooded valley.

"Here!" called one of the men. "There is Lin's shoe."

They found no other trace of Lin so returned home in great sadness.

But the dragon had got a taste for children. Soon, three more disappeared.

"Yen," called the villagers, "something must be done. We cannot survive with this dragon terrorising us every day."

Yen stroked his long grey beard and pondered for a moment.

"Who will volunteer to kill this dragon?" he demanded loudly.

No one spoke. The menfolk lowered their eyes and stared at the ground, shuffling.

"No one?" called Yen angrily. "Then I must think more deeply," he announced and went into his home.

When the sun at last **crept** above the rim of the volcano, he again struck the bell and called a meeting. Everyone gathered and there was a great murmuring and shuffling among the men, while the women gathered in small clusters, some weeping and others clutching their children tightly.

Yen held a black bag aloft so that all could see it.

"Within this bag there is a pebble for every one of you," he told them. "One by one, you must pull a pebble out of the bag. All the pebbles are white except one. Whoever pulls the green pebble from the bag will be the one chosen by fate to rid us of this dragon!"

Oh! There was such a noise within the meeting room when he had spoken! People rushed around, speaking to their friends and neighbours and arguing for and against the Wise Man's words until at last they grew quiet and began to line up before Yen. Each one took a pebble from the bag, even the children, and sighed with relief when they held up a white pebble, until it was the turn of twelve-year-old Mai-ling. She came forward nervously and put her hand in the bag, closing her eyes and pulling out a pebble. She held her hand up to the Wise Man and slowly opened her fingers. There, sitting on her small white palm, was a shiny green pebble.

"Mai-ling is the Chosen One!" called Yen.

The villagers all cheered and clapped Mai-ling on her back, saying, "Well done!" "What an honour!" "You must be so proud!" each relieved that it was she and not they who held the green pebble.

Although she was quaking inside, Mai-ling left the meeting hall and set off for the volcano, but when she reached the edge of the village she sat down on a rock, hanging her head in despair.

"What am I to do?" she cried aloud. "How can I slay a great big dragon? I'm only twelve." And she began to sob bitterly.

"Dry your eyes, child. Your sobbing disturbs my peace."

Mai-ling looked up, and through her tears saw an old man.

"I didn't see you," she said. "I am sorry. I will go." And she stood up to leave.

"Wait," said the man. "Tell me why you weep so hard."

Despite his stern voice and frowning face, Mai-ling found herself telling him all about Yen, the dragon and the trouble in the village.

"But that doesn't explain why you weep so hard," he answered. "Do you think weeping will help you overcome a dragon? No, it will not. Remember the ancient Chinese proverb 'Where there's a will there's a way.' Dry your eyes and I will tell you the secrets known only to Dragon Slayers!"

Mai-ling obeyed and sat down again. She was suddenly very curious about this strange old man. He was extremely tall and thin, clad in long black and white robes and his face was unsmiling, but there was something in his voice that gave her hope.

"As you know, dragons are covered in thick hard scales," he began. "No knife, sword or dagger can penetrate their armour. But there is one weakness. Under their heads, where the chin joins the throat there is a soft spot. That is where you must strike. One thrust of a silver dagger will kill him."

"But I don't have a silver dagger!" Mai-ling butted in.

"The final secret I shall tell you concerns the one thing that dragons fear," he continued as if she hadn't spoken. "Magpies! Dragons hoard the treasure that they have stolen all their lives. They believe that if a magpie steals one tiny bit from the hoard, their power to breathe fire will be lost forever." He chuckled. "It isn't true of course, but they are stupid brutes with very small brains inside their big skulls." Strangely, the sound of his laughter reminded Mai-ling of the cackling of magpies.

He reached beneath his black and white robe and brought out a shining silver dagger.

"You will need this," he said, handing it to her. "Now, have courage, travel quietly and watch out for magpies!"

With those words, he turned and melted away into the woods and she heard his strange cackling sound slowly fading as he disappeared.

Mai-ling held up the dagger. As a **beam** of sunlight shone through the clouds and struck it, she felt courage warming her blood and so, heartened, she set off on her quest. For two days, she crept cautiously up the side of the volcano. At last she neared the topmost rim and stopped to rest. Now so near, she looked up into the overcast sky, then back, down at the tiny village **nestling** in the foothills and her courage left as suddenly as it had come. The silver dagger felt cold in her hand and, in the shadows, seemed nothing more than an ordinary knife.

But she couldn't turn back now. She crept on. Loose stones **rattled** beneath her step. She stopped, listened, hardly daring to breathe. Nothing… She put her hands onto the rim of the volcano and peeped slowly over. There in the crater, coiled on a **bed** of gold and silver treasure, lay the enormous green dragon. His eyes were closed and the emerald-green armour of his scaly chest rose and fell with the rhythm of his breathing. His whole body, from his head down to the arrow-shaped tip of his long tail was covered in emerald-green scales. The massive veined wings were folded along his back, their usual lustre dulled by the overcast sky. His colossal jaw rested on a pillow of golden coins and from his nostrils, wisps of dragon-smoke spiralled up to join the grey clouds.

"Under the jaw," Mai-ling repeated beneath her breath, "between chin and throat. How can I lift your head though? How can I reach it?"

She began to crawl slowly, silently forward, her heart thumping so hard

ɟnt wake the dragon.

don't wake," went round

in her mind.

as she came close to the

ɔrmous head, a great cackling
noise broke the silence. Mai-ling's eyes
widened in horror as a flock of glistening
black and white magpies suddenly flew
overhead, flapping and cackling around the dragon. The dragon woke.
With a roar, he lifted his head and sent a burst of flame up into the sky.
Mai-ling struck. The dragon's jaw was pointing to the sky and there was
the soft weak spot, clearly visible between the chin and throat. She plunged
the silver dagger in as far as she could. The dragon stopped. He turned his
head. His small red eyes found Mai-ling and he opened his mouth. She
thought in an instant that she'd be overcome with searing flame, but the
dragon let out a deep groan and his head dropped with a clatter back onto
the pile of golden coins, sending them spinning and glittering around the
crater. The dragon was slain.

Mai-ling whirled around in a mad dance of joy as the magpies swooped
and dived onto the treasure, pulling small coins, rings and jewels from it
with their beaks and claws.

"Thank you! Thank you!" she called, laughing with triumph and relief.

She sat and watched the birds swirling over the dead dragon's hoard as
her heartbeat calmed. Then she rose and made her way down the side of
the volcano and back to Yishan.

As she approached, the villagers came to meet her. They cheered loudly
and lifted her high on their shoulders. Carrying her into the village, they
cried over and over, "Mai-ling — Dragon Slayer!"

Yen had left the village in shame after he had sent Mai-ling to kill the
dragon. On her return, the villagers held a meeting. They all decided that
she should be the village Wise Woman but Mai-ling was reluctant to agree.

"I am only a young girl," she said. "How can I be a village Elder?"

"You have great wisdom and courage," they insisted. "You alone slayed the dragon. It is your reward and your duty."

So Mai-ling became the village Elder and she struck the ancient bronze bell to announce a day of celebration. The villagers decorated the streets and their homes with red paper lanterns and they danced and sang late into the night.

Mai-ling's first act was to send a party of strong men up the volcano to bring back the dragon's treasure and so Yishan grew wealthy and prosperous. The villagers were glad to have such a wise young woman as their village Elder, and Mai-ling began to enjoy it too. Time passed slowly and easily in the village. Mai-ling grew taller, crops grew well and the people of Yishan thrived.

Until one day an ogre moved into the woods nearby.

"How can I defeat an ogre?" pondered Mai-ling. Then she remembered the stranger's wise words.

"Oh well," she said. "Where there's a will there's a way..."

The Kraken

What is the kraken?

Myth: A terrible creature appearing from the bubbling waters of the bottomless seas to devour man?

Or fact: A super squid with a bad reputation that inhabits the loneliest outreaches of our oceans?

The Kraken is a legendary sea monster of extraordinary size, which is said to have lived off the coasts of Norway and Iceland. It appears in ancient Norse stories and is central to many mariners' tales. It was supposedly able to attack a ship by wrapping its arms around the hull and dragging it and the sailors down to a watery grave.

Fishermen feared and respected the Kraken as they believed that huge amounts of fish gravitate around it and those who dared to fish above a sleeping Kraken could reap catches of epic proportion…so long as they didn't wake it!

This most fearsome beast was immortalised in the book *20,000 Leagues Under the Sea* by Jules Verne. It has appeared in poems, stories and most recently in the popular film *Pirates of the Caribbean.*

But where have these fantastical stories come from and is there any fact in them, or is it all fiction?

Myth or reality?

The Kraken of legend could well be a member of the species called cephalopod, most probably the giant squid or colossal squid. These squid live deep in remote waters and are seldom spotted. Scientists observing both types of super squid confirm that they are very aggressive so they could be the reality behind the Kraken myth.

Some scientists think that the reported Kraken attacks on ships are the result of mistaken identity. This is because the squids' natural enemy is the sperm whale and scientists know that sperm whales hunt both the giant and colossal squid. The squid defend themselves using weapons on their tentacles, which leave cuts on the whales. Therefore it could be that a squid seeing the whale-like shape of a boat above them is spurred on to fight what it mistakenly thinks is an enemy.

Squid facts

- Only a handful of giant squid and colossal squid have ever been seen. This is because they live at extreme depths of around 2200 metres and rarely surface.

- Reports differ, but scientists believe that colossal squid grow up to 20 metres long. They are the world's largest invertebrate.

- The colossal squid has razor-sharp hooks, which shred its prey. The giant squid has circular serrated sucker rings.

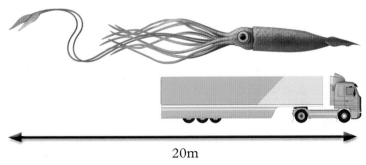

20m

Scientists belive colossal squid can grow to around 20 metres – longer than a lorry!

- The eyes of colossal squid are about 27 centimetres long and are believed to be the largest eyes in the animal kingdom.

- Both squid hunt large deep-sea fish, other squid and marine worms.

- They are the main food of the sperm whale.

The colossal squid has the largest eye of any animal.

Timeline

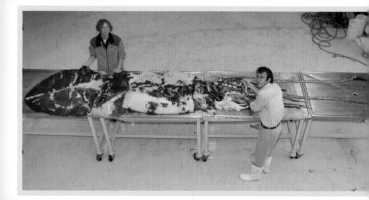

This colossal squid is a young adult – it is not yet fully grown!

AD730 -1066 Norse stories feature sea monster called the Kraken

1802 French biologists identify two new types of squid now known as the giant squid and the colossal squid

1930s *The Brunswick*, a tanker in the Royal Norwegian Navy, apparently attacked by a giant squid

1940s Giant squid reportedly attacks British sailors and their boat during Second World War

1925 First recovery of parts of the colossal squid in the stomach of a sperm whale

2003 First whole colossal squid (young adult) found in Southern Antarctica measuring 6 metres

2007 Largest colossal squid specimen to date captured off Antarctica measuring around 12 metres and weighing 450 kilograms

A Dragon Spotter's Guide to the Chinese Lung Dragon

The Chinese Lung dragon is the most common of the ancient Oriental dragons and therefore the ideal subject for a young dragon spotter. The other dragons of the region are the Korean Yong dragon, the Tibetan dragon and the Lindworm dragon, found in the Asian interior. See map below for distribution.

Ancient dragon distribution in Asia

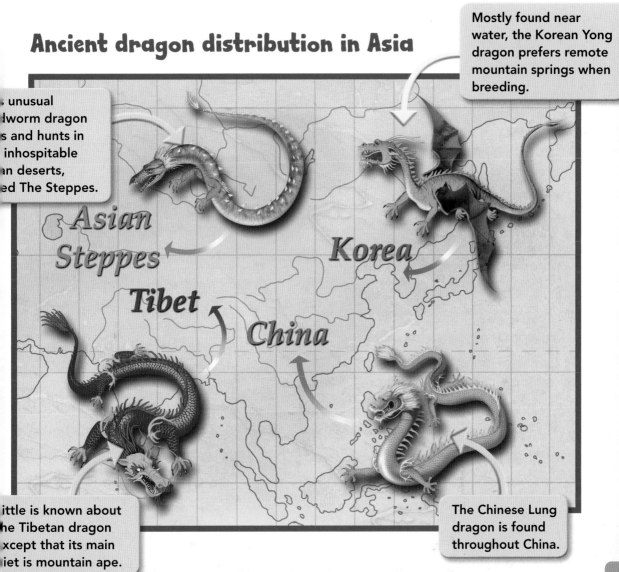

Mostly found near water, the Korean Yong dragon prefers remote mountain springs when breeding.

[...]s unusual [Lin]dworm dragon [...]s and hunts in [...] inhospitable [Asi]an deserts, [call]ed The Steppes.

Asian Steppes

Korea

Tibet

China

[L]ittle is known about [t]he Tibetan dragon [e]xcept that its main [d]iet is mountain ape.

The Chinese Lung dragon is found throughout China.

Anatomy of the Chinese Lung dragon

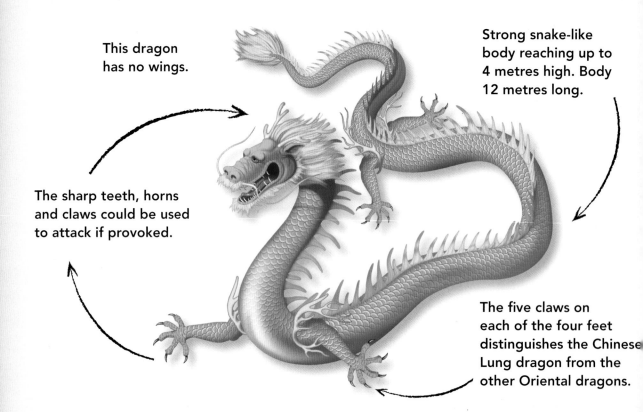

This dragon has no wings.

Strong snake-like body reaching up to 4 metres high. Body 12 metres long.

The sharp teeth, horns and claws could be used to attack if provoked.

The five claws on each of the four feet distinguishes the Chinese Lung dragon from the other Oriental dragons.

Where to search for the Chinese Lung dragon

The Chinese Lung dragon has a well-documented relationship with water. Indeed this dragon is closely associated with rain and many Chinese rivers are believed to have been formed by the original Dragon Kings from which they get their names. The Chinese Lung dragon that you may well spot is a direct descendant of these god-like creatures and although smaller and unable to do magic they are no less formidable.

The ideal Chinese Lung dragon habitat is secluded and close to water – either a river or lake. Its lair will undoubtedly be inaccessible, as these dragons tend to hide away in underwater caves or grottos. The keen dragon spotter needs to search for signs of dragon activity and then camp out to wait for the dragon.

What to look for

The Chinese Lung dragon mainly feeds on fish and birds so bones may be found near its lair. One of the most reliable indicators of the Chinese Lung dragon's presence is the enormous amount of dung that it produces. This is unmistakeable in both size and odour (which is something like rotten fish soup!). Once you have established that you are in the right area look for further signs such as scratch marks at shoulder height in trees, and claw prints. Remember that this species of dragon has five claws on each of its four feet.

Top Tips for sticky situations

Occasionally a dragon spotter can come upon a Chinese Lung dragon unawares. In this case the dragon might react aggressively because it is very wary of humans. These Top Tips will help the dragon spotter caught in a tight spot!

- All dragons love treasure so keep some shiny jewel-like objects to throw – they will distract a charging Chinese Lung dragon.
- Never get between a Chinese Lung dragon and water. If threatened the Chinese Lung dragon will retreat to water rather than attack.
- If all else fails climb a very high tree and stay there. This is safe because the Chinese Lung dragon cannot fly and will soon lose interest and leave the area.

Father's Day
Lou Kuenzler

Characters (in order of appearance)

- Cameron – an 11-year-old boy
- Ria – an 11-year-old girl
- Lorraine – Ria's mum
- Steve – Cameron's dad

Scene 1

It is the third Saturday in June. Cameron comes charging into the kitchen. Ria runs close behind, holding onto his T-shirt, trying to stop him getting there first.

Cameron	Lorraine! Lorraine!
Ria	Mum! Muuuuuuuuuuuuuuuuum!
Lorraine	What now?
Cameron	Ria won't let me on the computer. She's been on there for hours.
Ria	He tried to push me off it! It's my computer!

Lorraine	When Cameron's here, you have to share the computer, Ria. You know that.
Ria	But I'm doing my homework!
Cameron	No, you're not. You're just emailing your friends about your new haircut!
Ria	How dare you read what I've got on screen! It's private. Mum, tell him he's not allowed to read my personal correspondence. It's against the law!
Cameron	Oh yeah? What law's that? The law of stupid stepsisters? Anyway, how can it be private correspondence when you said it was your homework?
Ria	It *was* my homework!

Cameron	No, it wasn't!
Ria	Yes, it was!
Cameron	No, it wasn't!
Ria	Yes, it was!
Lorraine	*(Walks down stage and speaks directly to the audience. As she talks Ria and Cameron freeze – their body language should show the anger they feel towards one another.)*

Don't mind the bickering. It's just family! Quite a complicated family, I suppose … like lots of families nowadays. Perhaps I'd better introduce everyone, that might make it easier. I'm Lorraine and that's Ria, my daughter. Her real dad lives in Spain but I split up with him about five years ago and I'm married to Cameron's dad now. He's called Steve and he's about to walk through the door with a packet of bird seed…

Steve	All right one and all? Are you ruffling each other's feathers already?
Cameron	Ria won't let me on the computer, Dad.
Ria	Because I'm doing my homework!
Cameron	No, you're not!
Ria	Yes, I am!
Cameron	No, you're not!
Lorraine	*(To the audience again)* Cameron normally lives with his mum – about two hours up the motorway from here – but he comes to visit us quite often at weekends, or his dad drives up there sometimes. I know I'm supposed to be a wicked stepmother and have terrible, **malicious** thoughts about him but, actually, I think Cameron's great!

71

Really I do! I love having him in the house… I just wish him and Ria could get along better. And Steve? Well, Steve always thinks that humour is going to solve everything! You know how dads – or *stepdads* – are sometimes? Watch this! (It never works, by the way.)

Steve I see it's all happiness in the nest today. Smiles everywhere!

Ria It's not my fault. It's just I've got homework to do.

Cameron Yeah, and I've got homework, too. It's called getting to Level 10 of Cyberspin 2020 before Jack Parker from my school.

Lorraine (To audience) Humour from him too, see – you can tell he's Steve's son!

Steve Well in that case I've got the perfect solution. Why don't we hop in the car right now and I'll drive you both to that huge electrical superstore on the edge of town. When we get there, I'll buy you each a brand new, shiny, state-of the-art laptop! You'll never have to share anything ever again.

Cameron Ha ha!

Ria Very funny!

Steve What? You don't believe me? Don't tell me you suspect that this is a cunning ruse to outwit you both?

Ria and Cameron Yes! We do!

Lorraine (To audience) Perhaps it does work, after all – at least they're agreed on something for once! Although, in truth, they both love Steve's **eccentricities**. That's half the problem … they vie for his attention even more than they fight over that screen!

Scene 2

Later the same day.

Lorraine	Have you two remembered it's Father's Day tomorrow? You should get Steve something.
Cameron	I know, let's jump in the car and drive down to that…
Ria	…huge electrical superstore on the edge of town…
Ria and Cameron	*(Laughing)* We could buy him a brand new, shiny, state-of-the-art laptop!
	(This time it is Ria who steps forward to talk to the audience as the others freeze.)
Ria	At least Cameron's being nice for once. Since Mum banned us both from the computer we're getting on much better. He can be a real laugh sometimes.
Cameron	Why should Ria get Steve anything? He's not her real dad!
Ria	*(To audience)* And then – surprise, surprise – he has to go and ruin it all!
Lorraine	Nobody said he was her dad, Cameron. But, being a stepdad is an important role too. Steve looks after Ria. He works hard to put food on our table and she has a lot to thank him for.
Ria	*(To Cameron)* I spend much more time with Steve than you do. I bet you don't even know what he's interested in at the moment, do you?
Cameron	Golf…?
Ria	Ha! My Father's Day present's going to be a big hit and yours will be a big miss!
Lorraine	Please, kids! Do try and stop this one-upmanship. Why don't you just tell us what you're going to get him, Ria? It might give Cameron some ideas.
Ria	I saw the perfect thing in the window of that gift shop in North Square.

Lorraine	The **quaint**, half-timbered place with all the floral porcelain and translucent glass?
	(Ria nods.)
Lorraine	What did you get him? A funny teapot?
Ria	*(To audience again)* Maybe! But I'm not saying anything more, otherwise Cameron might steal my idea. He's so misguided, thinking Steve's still keen on golf. His new craze is birdwatching. He feeds them in the garden all the time, then treks off on long country walks with his binoculars. "Ornithological expeditions," he calls them…whatever that means! I saw this perfect plate in the window of the gift shop. It's got a beautiful kingfisher on it – all blue and green and gold. Steve's been trying to spot a kingfisher down by the weir all summer but he hasn't seen one yet. I reckon the plate will make up for that a bit! He can look at it every morning when he eats his toast. Better still, Cameron will probably get him some rubbish golf tees or something!
Steve	*(Walks through heading straight for the garden)* All right my little fledgelings? What are you all plotting?
Lorraine, Ria and Cameron	Nothing!
Ria	Nothing at all!

Scene 3

Late afternoon. Ria is sitting at the kitchen table crying her eyes out while Lorraine tries to comfort her. Cameron is pacing up and down.

Ria I hate you!

Cameron *(To the audience as the others freeze.)*
I guess it's no surprise! I did steal her idea for a Father's Day gift. I went to the shop in North Square and saw the kingfisher plate right away. Personally, I think it's horrifically ugly. The lady in the shop said the colours were gorgeous… But they just look really girlie to me! All gold and turquoise. Yuk!

Lorraine You have been **devious**, Cameron, going behind Ria's back.

Cameron I said I'm sorry a hundred times. What else can I do?

Ria You can go home! That's what you can do!

Lorraine Ria! This is Cameron's home, even though he doesn't live here all the time.

Cameron Why don't you go away for once, Ria? Why don't you go to Spain and visit your own dad?

Ria *(Crying even louder)* Don't you dare talk about my dad!

Cameron *(To audience)* I really shouldn't have said that. Ria never gets to see her real dad. He runs a vineyard in a remote part of Spain and it takes ages to get there from here. He's bitter about the divorce, too. At least my mum and dad still communicate. He refuses to speak to Lorraine at all, even about arrangements, so everything is always supremely complicated.

Lorraine Cheer up, Ria! Don't let Steve see you crying today.

Ria I don't care what Steve sees. He's only my stupid stepdad. I hate him anyway!

Lorraine	That's not true.
Ria	*(To Cameron)* All because of you, I had to buy Steve this stupid mug.
Cameron	*(Reads)* WORLD'S BEST DAD!
Lorraine	That's lovely.
Cameron	Yeah, what's wrong with that?
Ria	You just don't get it, do you?
Cameron	*(To audience)* Is this one of those girl things?
Ria	You stole my kingfisher plate!
Cameron	I didn't steal it. I went into the shop and paid good money for it.
Ria	You stole my idea! You knew that's what I wanted to give Steve.
Cameron	No, I didn't. You wouldn't tell anyone, remember? You did your whole secret agent espionage routine.
Ria	You worked it out. This can't be a coincidence.
Cameron	*(To audience)* She's right, of course. But only because she was being so smug. I think she hoped I'd give him some kind of golf present. Just because she lives here – with my dad – she thinks she knows more about him than I do. It's so obvious he's into birdwatching. He'd nest in a tree and grow a beak if he could! As soon as I saw the kingfisher plate, I knew that's what Ria had her eye on. Still, I suppose it was a pretty spiteful thing to do.
Ria	Now I can't give Steve anything.
Lorraine	What about the mug? WORLD'S BEST DAD! He'll be really touched that's how you feel about him.
Ria	But I don't feel that! He's not the "world's best dad". Not to me. That's why I'm crying…
Cameron	*(To audience)* Now I'm totally confused!

Ria   I really love Steve. He's great. But the best dad in the world, for me, is my real dad. I feel so disloyal.

Cameron   Why don't you send the mug to your dad, then?

Lorraine Father's Day in Spain is in March. They celebrate on a different day to Britain.

Ria   And I wouldn't have anything to give Steve. I don't hate him really, I want to give him something special…

Cameron   *(To audience)* Maybe there is a way I can sort this out!

Scene 4

It's Father's Day. Steve has unwrapped his presents and is smiling broadly. The others all talk at once.

Lorraine Happy Father's Day, darling.

Ria   Happy Father's Day, Steve.

Cameron   Happy Father's Day, Dad.

Steve   Thank you! How about some coffee in my mug and some toast on my plate? I can't be bottom of the pecking order today, you know!

Lorraine We'd better indulge him, I suppose.

         (The others freeze as Steve turns to talk to the audience.)

Steve   I was really touched by all this. It's not easy being a stepdad and a real dad, too. I know half the time Cameron thinks Ria is a cuckoo pushing him out of the nest; and Ria thinks Cameron is a buzzard, swooping down to pick her out of the way. In reality, there's plenty of room for them both.

Did you see what Ria gave me? This beautiful plate. *(He holds it up.)* See how **iridescent** the colours are? Fancy Ria knowing I'd been trying to spot that kingfisher down by the weir.

And Cameron gave me this mug. I'm so moved – WORLD'S BEST DAD! I thought he was cross with me for not living with his mum anymore, for being here with Lorraine and Ria, so it meant the WORLD for me to read that!

Cameron   You haven't looked at our card yet, Dad.

Ria   Cameron and I made it for you together.

Cameron   On the computer.

Ria   At the same time!

Steve   *(Pretending to faint)* Knock me down with a feather! Who'd have thought it… My nestlings, sharing the computer. What next?